Words of Healing
Letter by Letter

Fazila Nurani

ISBN: 978-1-7782914-0-1

Published in Canada by Pandamonium Publishing House™.
www.pandamoniumpublishing.com

Cover Design: Alex Goubar
alexgoubar.com

CONTENTS

Dear Reader,

I am deeply grateful for this opportunity to celebrate words with you!

It is often said that when a person has a direct experience of some form of awakening, or an unworldly jolt that leaves them deeply touched by the sanctity of life, it is very difficult to put such a profound realization into words. Language can never do justice to matters of the spirit, but I am honoured in this introduction to my A-Z book of poems to share my story, as best as I possibly can, on how this offering came about.

My inward adventure occurred almost three years ago on March 13th, 2019, and it shook me to the core. It was during my visit to the Rythmia Life Advancement Centre in Costa Rica. I journaled every moment of this 'event' but without ever going back to read about it, I remember it vividly, as if it was yesterday. The profound connection I felt to every sound and sight in the ceremony room during the third night of my stay at Rythmia will be with me forever. This innate knowing that my life is orchestrated, that everything is unfolding just as it is meant to, regardless of what I do or try to control, was not a knowing in my head but was vibrating through my entire being. It gave a new meaning to books I had read and thought I understood such as Jon Kabat-Zinn's *Falling Awake*, Byron Katie's *Loving What Is* or Matt Liticia's *The Path is Everywhere*.

What was most interesting, looking back, is how I longed to communicate this experience immediately afterwards. With a burning heart, the words just flowed freely from a place I had never spoken from before. My mind had been hushed – there was literally a gap in thought as I spoke. It was as if some greater power was speaking through me and within me. I had this visceral sense of being steered, while completely interdependent with the ground beneath my feet and the moon hanging overhead.

After days of digesting this mystery, I still desperately wanted to put words to the experience, even if verbalizing it would be extremely challenging. I often received blank stares or looks of confusion. Slowly but surely, time carried on as it does, and I stopped talking about my Rythmia experience, but kept it tucked in my heart, pulling it out during quiet moments to myself.

Then, as if on cue, I re-discovered poetry. I was moved to tears by simple short translations of verses written by early mystic poets:

Kabir on happiness:

> Ever since happiness heard your name,
> it has been running through the streets
> trying to find you…

Rumi on grace:

> Surrender to grace.
> The ocean cares for each wave until it reaches the shore.
> You are given more help than you will ever know.

Kahlil Gibran on sorrow:

> The deeper that sorrow carves into your being,
> the more joy you can contain.

My gentle late father would often quote Rumi so I was somewhat familiar with mystic poets. Craving to better know works written in English rather than translated, I started my search for modern poets and discovered the power and raw beauty of poems written by Jane Hirshfield, David Whyte and others. I was inspired to write myself – both reading and writing poetry became a meditation for me.

The poems contained in this book are reflections on my personal experiences and thoughts, as these have been my inspiration. I think of them as a celebration of, and a blessing to, words. It is a sacred practice for me to write poetry that could support another's connection to their deeper self, and my hope is that you will find in this book some content that is meaningful, healing and inspirational for you personally.

ETYMOLOGY AND THIS COLLECTION OF POEMS

I distinctly remember how much I loved reading aloud when I was eight years old. A paperback dictionary was always perched beside me, well before the days of the Internet and digital searches. I had to stop at any word I didn't know to look it up, and then would wander away from the unfinished page until I felt I had the new word memorized. I have been attracted to expanding my vocabulary as long as I can remember. I also believe having a breadth of words to choose from has assisted my professional life as a lawyer by allowing me to communicate more precisely. Even ordinary words when used in the right context can produce extraordinary sentences.

Language, a key communication tool, appears to take off with a life of its own. It evolves. As time goes on, new words are incorporated into our vocabularies, and old words are either forgotten and made obsolete or otherwise reappropriated, adapted to the current era, where they then undergo subtle changes of meaning. Over the years I have become increasingly fascinated with etymology, the study of the origin of words. Words have the ability to open up worlds for us when we communicate, and original meanings are powerful pointers to the emotions that words can trigger. By way of example, the word 'sad' comes from an Indo-European root *satis*, being 'enough' (satisfied). Although the meaning changed in Middle English to sorrowful, by knowing its origin one can relate sadness to a gratifying sense of tenderness, a fullness of heart.

I use the Online Etymology Dictionary written and compiled by Douglas Harper regularly. As expected, the historical view on words is often diverse. Whether the word came from Latin, Old or Middle English; was influenced by German, French or Italian; or was borrowed from Greek or Hebrew, are matters of differing opinion and some contention.

This book connects my love of poetry with my keen interest in etymology. Each poem essentially explores the genesis of common words that start with each letter of our modern English alphabet. The focus word(s) are *italicized* followed by a way in which this word was originally used in **[bold]**. Even if it were possible, accuracy is not my goal. I seek to convey an appreciation of how the word was once used and how, just maybe, knowing this illuminates our understanding of it.

In memory of my dear father, Salim Moosa, a storyteller, a lover of words

Listen to presences inside poems
Let them take you where they will.

Follow those private hints,
and never leave the premises.

- Rumi

Radical Act of Bravery

the word *alone* **[All + One]** stands by itself
like an imminent threat of loneliness
a dark path to being left   left alone

Abandonment. Alienation. Abnegation.

yet all alone we belong   fully ourselves
invited to embrace our inner voice
no one can experience my aching heart for me
feel the rain on my skin
or live the thoughts that I think

we
     came into this world alone
     will leave it alone
even together we are alone
encouraged to cultivate
the rawest intimacy   with aloneness

around the buzzing meeting table
on an over-crowded beach
even in the happiest committed relationship
inhabiting aloneness is possible
and perhaps even necessary

like the wise old trees   those breathtaking giants
I marvel at how they reach up to the sky
mighty and strong   with ease and grace
a trust in aloneness as the forest
communes in stillness

to let myself and others alone
is to accept how we each show up
to enjoy myself alone is a celebration
not a fate to which I have been condemned

to embody the solitude of human existence
at the very core of profound connection
is a radical act   of bravery

Tick Tock

there is a story that visits often:
"you're running out of time"
demanding I multi-task or just go faster
but to escape the prison of time
is to grant the hours their own life

a miracle follows sharp stinging winter
out of the dead garden rises
overwhelming abundance
minutes like seasons sometimes
flowering other times withering

today arrives because of each step taken
      by my ancestors
      by my past selves
the future will arrive with insights gained
      from an aching heart
      from this mind I train

stone people, plant people, four-legged
creepy crawlers, finned and winged ones
why do you not see the clock?

infinite possibilities in this moment
distress only showing up in another
precious container of TIME
holds this fragile life lightly
to support us as we press on

when I *bless* **[praise]** the days given
in turn the seconds bless me back
each one a tiny treasure with a gap between
graciously expanding as I stop counting
tick…

C - CONFUSION, COURAGE

Closer

[Ek maan: one mind]
I grew up with guilt. Rushing to catch up
with religious ceremonies. Missing the call to prayer
my mindscape never ready for these invocations, this
structure, these rituals. Sneaking into prayer hall
lateness longing to hide from critical stares. Anxious
eyes open but told they shouldn't be. Fight
distraction! Focus on the meaning
of these Arabic words

[thobha thobha: I repent, I repent]
Every day a call to prayer. No pressure if
too busy but lost opportunity makes me weary
could be a jackpot – pray for good grades,
a boyfriend, enlightenment, forgiveness. Ah yes,
forgiveness on repeat: O Lord! I am a sinful person
if the congregation forgives me God will forgive
me – soul cleansed. Relieved
start again

Guilty [gyltig: offending, delinquent]
But I kept committing many a bad deed – like when
wallet forgotten, I decided to steal that t-shirt
or the time I cheated on that science exam
lied to make my life appear more interesting
violated the no alcohol rule – it's a sin
to even think about suicide right?

[Siratu-al-Mustaqim: right path]
Precious little boy a quick study
Arabic prayers rolling off his tongue. Time to
learn the meanings so it all makes sense:
Guide us to the path of the favored ones – not of
those cursed ones and nor of those who have gone
astray – taken aback by the question: Who
are the cursed ones? More surprised by my answer:
Well, everyone who isn't on the same path ofcourse
he looks up with eyes wide: Like my bestest friend

Matthew cuz he don't know the prayers?
I fumble: No, no! like the ones who do bad things
he glances down at his slipping sock, a heel partly
exposed: But you say me making mistakes is okay...

Confusion
[cōnfundere: to mingle together]
this wildly disorienting off-balance moment
mingles with the hypocrisy of it all. I drop everything
right there shaking, down on my knees
face to face with my son
drop prayer, drop congregation, drop Arabic teachings
guilt shows its ugly face as weeks and months go
by wringing my neck, suffocating me with community
whispers, unspoken disapproval:
You're on the wrong path, failing your kids
come back!
Am I the ultimate sinner doomed
for hardship and hell?

Courage **[cor: from heart]**
to inch forward towards
a connection back to self
Open. Curious. Perceiving wisdom
beyond the faith I grew up in
treasured and struggled in
for 30 years now an outsider looking in
to customs and traditions – who knew?
honouring everyone practicing humanity
oblivious to their chosen community
guilt being the hell I peeled off
the confining skin I shed

closer to God than ever

Letting Be

yesterday a carefree child
bouncing wide-eyed excitement
today a guarded teen
overcome by overwhelming emotions
      diving in, I seek to rescue
      fix – solve – set the path forward
      only to find a path
      not mine to set

stumbling at times
soaring at others
I pull back as you grow forward
here to lean on when you're ready
      what if you never come back
      what if you don't need me any more
      could shattered dreams break you
      sadness swallow you whole?

deliberate **[un-freeing possibilities to discover
the actuality]** letting go
forcing myself to honour your footprints
      trusting our feet to lead

only then when it feels like
you are miles away
you come running back
for a shoulder to cry on
      your journey disconnecting from mine
      like a railcar longing for its own track
      your path reconnecting with mine
      meandering tracks merging

we parent each other and ourselves
from clinging and controlling
      to soothing and surrendering
      a sigh of relief for what the winds deliver

The Unwanteds

solitary oyster secretes nacre
organic matter neatly layered
sacred experiences, stronger than concrete
dulling over time when dry
moisture of new hurts seduce
those unwanteds to shine again
not enoughness, shame
abandonment, rejection
together in our apartness

in my blood
        anxious journey across continents
in my bones
        two steps behind but longing to be noticed
somatic memories stored in the body
unmet needs packed firmly

I can feel my mother's pain when I am still
and the grief of her mother
I shed the tears they held back
when rain pours the skies open
to weep for us all…rivers
upon rivers to water this planet
this ache a predicament of being alive
fragile moments gifted to us all
I saw it in the eyes of a racoon
hobbling on a broken limb
I saw it in the mighty tree tipping
sap bleeding from shock of chainsaw
let's *explore* **[cryout]** together

I watch the unwanteds closely
as they shine again I embrace them
even as they chip and flake off
just by no longer rejecting these hurts
just by holding them in loving kindness

brilliant how a lifetime of wounds layer
longing to be seen and integrated
rather than abandoned
each coating an invitation:
immerse yourself in messages
carried – liberation promised
at the very centre of this precious pearl

Drenched

the things I should have said,
the ways in which I turned away
protecting an image I never was
for a salvation I never knew

> *– Jeff Foster, **"A Perfect Love"***

as you lash out with disgust
words come pouring out
spilling daggers uncontained
as I fight to stay afloat
in rising waters of pain
knowing these words cannot be *forgotten* **[lost]**
even if *forgiven* **[giving up desire to punish]**
replaceable by "thank you for your opinion"
if I was in control, but it is too late for
the things I should have said

these words that took a life of their own
you ugly man, you fucking asshole
echo relentlessly in my mind
undercurrent of anger and shame
pulls me down deeper still
as I gasp and choke on the bitterness
taunting – see how mean you can be?
desperate for recovery but
drowning a real threat now because of
the ways in which I turned away

a familiar place to the child I once was
craving to be accepted, celebrated
even when mistaken, naughty or nasty
just as it was, just as I am
an attempt to scramble to shore
escape feelings of unworthiness
justify these words stubbornly
with more words designed to convince you
of the law – cause and effect only
protecting an image I never was

the one who craves to be right on the surface
but has already let herself down below it
let there be hurting let the suffering
I've earned wash over me
it's the only way out of here
storm subsiding on the other side
water surface calm and still for now
no longer fighting for air
redeeming the holiness of relationship
for a salvation I never knew

The basic premise of the Glosa (a medieval Spanish poetic form) is as follows: Four lines of poetry are quoted as an epigraph from another poem. These four lines act as a refrain in the final line of four stanzas, each 10 lines in length. The Glosa feels like a celebration of another poet! You will find another Glosa at letter Z in this book.

Lucid

in the obscure darkness
with blankets embracing
      I end the day by turning in
      the only place to go

thoughts transmute and garble as I drop
from light slumber to a deep unknown
      moments of waking till sunrise
      to revisit familiar tones

as ripples of the heart and mind leave clues
riddles on the surface of the stillest pond
      hazy visions dance on and on
      forgotten before remembered

and then for the first time
      I *glimpse* **[shine, glisten]**, alert

perched on the mountain's summit
illuminated by glorious sunlight
      infinite blue skies in all directions
      a surreal awareness I am dreaming

I could fly   I could dive
into the vast green valleys below
      instead this thrill rouses me
      from a place I long to know

where do we go in the night?
the dark carrying us away to create
      falling asleep again and again
      in hopes of falling awake

Melt

dangling icicles glitter in the sun
droplets swell, cling, quiver and finally free fall
splattering, disappearing into wet pavement

letting go – I take myself less seriously now
cracking up always feels better
finding *humor* **[fluids of the body]**

flexible and adaptable in the liquid state
fitting into any container of experience
life throws my way unexpectedly

rigid and stubborn in the solid state
easily bent out of shape when push comes to shove
the very source of such suffering

grace always here in the vapor state – hidden
presence can be felt like the stars in the sky
looking so solid these hot balls of gas

shining, shimmering   heavenly bodies
pointing to the children we once were and the elders
we are becoming, encouraging us

to see how we are one and the same
whether frozen solid or going with the flow
the more solid the set up the greater the joke

as we play this game of being human
not a guarded giggle but an uncontrollable roar
cracking the edges of our personalities

*A version of this poem was originally published in Understorey Magazine's Issue 20 (2021):
Laughter understoreymagazine.ca*

Wiser

blinding lights, frigid air
disconnected with a snip of the cord
longing for cocoon of warm soothing waters
persistent persuasion to seek comfort on my own
find lungs, voice box, hands, without being shown
Overwhelmed

               … as *intended* **[stretched toward]**

numbers, letters, use your words
that stuffed giraffe is MINE!
too much noise – too busy – too scary
bawling in anticipation of whatever's next
disapproving glare, ashamed I am a pest
Rejected

               … as intended

tucking hurts of childhood into corners
a voice tells me: not good enough,
say it better. look better. be better.
you like my image but do you like ME? this imperfect one
who throbs and yearns – the one you do not see?
Exhausted

               … as intended

choose wisely. what are you good at?
find your passion – the impact you'll make
resigning to priorities defined by others
here comes the one who will save me! fix me! make me whole!
romance fades patterns of blame take their toll
Resisting

               … as intended

unprepared caretaker for this tiny fragile being
no manual no course no experience
not a perfect parent. be kinder. try harder.
desperate need to be liked by this precious child
shadows increasingly difficult to hide
Guilty

               … as intended

their own personalities, their own dreams
left with my marriage, my career, a desperate need
to dig deeper. step back. put life in perspective
spacious pauses no longer equal laziness
smell of danger fading as I embrace life's tests
Self-care

               --- as intended

expecting many detours along the way
the path itself now seen as such grace
Wiser

               … with *intention* **[an act of stretching]**

Dear Body...

my younger self despised you
called you awkward when you needed care
seized you in mirror with an angry glare
yet you steadily guided me as I grew
supported my path and yes, still do
now I *justify* **[make right]** hurts you bear
with this gratitude each day shared
I am driven to a much kinder view

thank you baby toe for teaching patience
when you broke and slowly healed
thank you skin, how you forgave
when burned you gently peeled
thank you legs, when pushed so hard
you pressed forward and did not yield

you stand up for me long bones
cradle anxious thought dear brain
cherished liver you diligently drain
toxins from blood all on your own
complex systems managing their zones
don't mind wrinkles and creakiness gained
I witness you carry me through joint pains
honouring how you've always known:

thank you gut for building my trust
in this sense of right from wrong
thank you tongue for speaking my truth
when I'm searching for how to belong
thank you heart, you relentlessly beat
now I know what it means to be strong

Go On... Stay

craving ground when we must go on
when nothing can stay
the same – human experience of
underlying restlessness   music
with its rhythm and moving stream of melody
not meant to be grasped by pausing or rewinding
not meant to be captured in head instead of heart
fluctuation in sounds gives vitality and
a terrifying threat to constancy

craving escape, an unwillingness to stay
with discomfort when under siege
this strong reaction to criticism a distraction
this habit of leaving – perhaps with
        alcohol
        shopping
        social media
        chocolate cake
        blaming, insulting
        aloofness, impatience
but wounds seek nurturing to heal

karma **[actions]**, auto-responses
cementing my nature if I fail to reflect

tiny seed goes on to become the giant oak tree
small spark stays to kindle a booming bonfire

learning
        when to go on   when to stay

Practice On

coming to mat with Grace
the body so wise
sets the intention for my hour here
I listen in stillness to its whisper
ready   now
to be moved by movement

coming to mat with Presence
the body a sacred temple
presses against heavy air
breath rising and falling deliberately
a gift to remember spirit wind

coming to mat to Bow to ourselves
challenging the body with a balancing pose
accepting how this container shows up today
limitations of hips and shoulders
acknowledged without expectation

dropping to knee cushions like a Child at play
surrendering to the force of gravity
this earth pulling me closer
guiding the body to rest - stillness
after motion that *longed* **[lengthened, extended]**

I have floated like a feather in the wind
stood like a tree reaching and rooting
anchored, twisted and fallen
a Practice – not perfection
each day a new body   a new mind
      brings fierce awareness to potential

a tickle brings me to my face
drip of sweat or trickle of a tear?
illusive end as the practice continues
chill of rotating fan over blanket of heat
goosebumps coaxing to stay a little longer
coming to mat to be cradled
a Quest Within…

In heartfelt appreciation for Sukha Yoga in Thornhill, Ontario, Canada and all boutique yoga studios/teachers everywhere who guide authentic yoga practices that encourage inner exploration during movement and stillness.

Perfectly Unfinished

he's waiting for you
my phone casually conveys on the tarmac
I already miss airplane mode
he can't breathe, they're intubating
an objection to terminating life support

if he can't get enough air on his own?
I wish we could buddy breathe with one regulator
breath held as we taxi to the gate
fingers tingling, ears ringing
panic quickly fills my lungs longing

for precious air, I've been here before
I felt it in a dream when being pulled underwater
      in a float tank deprived of all sound and light
         in a sweat lodge as the heavy space closed in
I woke up, opened the lid, darted for the exit

but you can't escape. Picturing you suffocate
battle for the breath you can not take
now I gaze at your fragile frame
being breathed in your ICU hospital bed
unexpectedly peaceful

wearing your identity like a loose garment
a shoe with more wiggle room, no longer stuck in your ways
as machines are shut off and all tubes detached
your gaping mouth invites cherished air – a force of habit
but the lungs finally surrender…its time

to go in this *moment* **[momentum; motion]**
of lengthening gap between breaths
even if your life is perfectly unfinished

A version of this poem was originally published in Third Lane Magazine's October 2021 issue.
thirdlanemag.com

Begin Again

drifting up from sleep as warm light peaks
into dark room at edges of blinds
unable to block newness of the day
calling to me to begin again

focusing on dream catcher hanging above
perfectly still to grasp fading memories
of dreams so real wrapped in strangeness
unnoticed a moment ago

garbage truck rumbles in the distance
slow to start – feet touching down
finding ground for the first time
ready to balance tasks of the day

silent kettle encouraged to boil
anxious sputter to confident rumble
many possibilities for how
I can unfold from the emptiness

pressing hopeful marks onto page
how this day should look without
clamor of preconceived ideas
fresh intentions invigorate me

every day an opportunity to *notice* **[notify]**
the one looking to learn: remaining
awestruck for the opportunity
to begin again…

Simple Gifts

large box delivered

today

peering longingly

treasure taller than she
waiting for emptiness

Waiting...
so she can climb in

vast container
private space

enclosing herself
safe

silent sanctuary

rain has been falling

for over an hour

street now full of

puddles calling
nothing could be more glorious than

Nothing...
ripples created

one giant leap
in shiny rubber boots

waves and whirlpools
oceans

beneath her

grassy field filled with

dandelion seeds

bobbing blowballs

like mini fireworks
gently she picks one

Gently....
then a sharp inhale

swollen cheeks
giant puff

scatters mini chutes
drifting

effortlessly away in the wind

fat candle burning

throws shadows on wall

mesmerizing flame

dancing freely
Watching...
watching wide-eyed
thick pool spreads

chubby finger dips in
stinging

squeal of delight
hardens

look! a finger glove!

Life delivers

ordinary **[orderly]** simple gifts

value from

pleasure not price

child within

longing to freely explore

Bittersweet

profound micro miracle
in a deep oasis of soothing echos
swoosh of warm blood flow
rhythmic drum of a heartbeat

a dear mother holds
space, dreamy infinite mystery
of shadows where sleep and wakefulness
melt together in this timeless floating cocoon

a body takes shape, preparing
for the journey to this mysterious world
consciousness itself sets the pace
for this fragile container of Life

such anticipation – then relief – then joy
in that room where the first cry is heard
where the lights are shockingly bright
and the air is dreadfully cold

we are born saying goodbye
what strength it took to leave!
this wail a vibrating reluctance to separate
from comforting embrace of the womb

how to belong – who to belong to?
tragic realization of *parting* **[being distinguished]**
to be heard, to be seen, to be found
somatic appreciation for connection

celebration…this first breath, bittersweet

Whispers

sometimes words spill unstoppable
downpour without pause
reverberating above the neck
an overpowering roar swallowing
surroundings, sucking me out
rehearsing the future   regurgitating the past
wreaking havoc until they exhaust me

sometimes there are no known words
for this, I must *quiet* [rest] to receive
subtle sensations below the neck
he tells me to clarify but meaning
is in the spaces between words
he tells me to describe it but do we ask
the blackbird why she sings her song?

these whispers playing hide-and-seek
lost in this moment...found in the next
telling me to live life   as a dance
                    feet moving without a destination
          by the stream
                    gently letting go of each passing ripple
          with the fire
                    no need to arrive in some final position

I remain humbly open to the unexpected
eruption of words – or no words
liberated from the shackles of:
          conformity and correctness
          the need to be liked or even heard
dear Spirit, I'm done chasing voices
whisper to me   lead me

R - REFLECT, RESPECT
Interaction

there she is again
an immediate reaction
pleasantly surprised or
somewhat disappointed
a longer interaction
with the one looking back
do these eyes gazing in my direction
see the face that you see?
is this image
really me?

this glass remains
ready to receive
unstained by whatever appears
no projection, just a calm consideration
static yet *reflecting* **[bending]**
without evaluation
like an alert deer
in the forest, aware
without ancient familiar habits
of likes and dislikes

now let's meet
somewhere beyond
not at the light rays bouncing
off these reified faces
an illusion
stopping at the packaging
feels comfortable until
this superficial interaction
no longer is…
Respect **[observe]** the call behind the mirror

Flip

there instead of here
then instead of now
another place, another time
unsettled with anticipation of
        next month
           next year
              next holiday

lodged in my throat
say that instead of this
do more instead of less
go instead of *staying* **[being]**
        other thoughts
           other words
              other actions
a disturbing lack of satisfaction

dis-ease makes me sick
                bubbles in a pancake ready to be flipped
locked in my mind
                stubbornly stuck to the pan
keeping Life arms-length away
                burning the underside of breakfast plans
reclaim and release
                flip

coulds and shoulds de-pressing me down
until my heart breathes:
        it's OK not to be okay
a yearning to hold space
        for resistance and acceptance
this moment beckoning me to *stay* **[be]**
        within this fragile peace

The Gardener

such potential this plot of land
where weeds spread so quickly
>> this mind full of tangled stories
>> deeply, stubbornly rooted

this tilling of the soil
gently removing invasive species
>> this tending to my thoughts
>> *trusting* **[making strong]** this being

soil too depleted for life-supporting plants
calling desperately for fertilizer, manure
>> underlying beliefs sucking energy
>> turning to poetry, saints and sages

over time, vegetables, medicinal plants,
flowers and fruit trees flourish
>> self-awareness carefully cultivated
>> as teachings and practice trickle down

from head to heart
the gardener recognizes
transformation isn't seen
in an afternoon of digging
it comes with a lifetime
of persistent attention

why is it I am
this self, who comes here *unique*
[only] visiting

in this school of life
the curriculum unfolds
unique **[sole]** journey

each of us *unique*
[one], unlike any other
precious chance to be
no same feather, snowflake, star
let's show up here as we are

Haiku: classic 17-syllable form of Japanese poetry constructed of three lines of 5-7-5 syllables

Tanka: classic 31-syllable form of Japanese poetry constructed of five lines of 5-7-5-7-7 syllables

Devotion

do I exist if you ignore me
rejected in this rigid cage
brittle expectations incite scarlet scars:

> you deserve better
> you know what's best
> this is good, that is bad
> they're the reason for this mess

you ache when sternum can't keep us apart
see, my tearing fibers are your north star
you long for chambers that no longer imprison me
celebrate! you've fallen apart completely

look no further to protect me from tragedy
you will come to know your capacity
to feel joy will be matched by your willingness
to dive into sacred sadness

when sharp word shards pierce my flesh
fracture lines erupt razor sharp and fresh
slowly turn in – resist the urge
to look outward for fault lines that merge
into the one who you beg to blame
attend to me instead, breathe in this pain
laser focused, get curious and dare
to devote yourself to my gentle care
for I am and always will be...
your *vulnerable* [wounded] heart

Tender Guide

the sun gives glorious light
its nature is not to
shine so brightly for itself

the rive gushes cleansing water
its nature is not to
flow freely to quench its own thirst

the tree bears delicate fruit
its nature is not to cling,
nourishing itself but to ripen and let fall

the lilac bursts with a sweet aroma
its nature is not to
contain fragrance but to drift beyond

the songbird sings an uplifting melody
its nature is not to
praise itself but the splendour all around

as nature gives and gives and gives again
unconditionally relentlessly
we bear witness to the way of compassion without
even a whisper of 'you owe me'

wait **[wake up, observe carefully]**
be taught now by the earth
our tender guide

Stranger on the Table

I appear more abundant on Mars
perhaps brought here from beyond
member of a noble family
though they thought I could never bond
mysterious trace, I remained in hiding
no odour no colour no taste
yet heavy and real I longed to be seen
in vacuum vessel abandoned as waste

first Ramsay found Lazy Argon
Shy Krypton reluctantly appeared
Neon boasted a brilliant red glow
nobel prize winning chemist steered
delicate work to behold my dazzling blue
months of fractional distilling needed
before enough of me was ready to be measured
what a joy to be seen and treated

as a rare treasured element [Stranger]
Xenon being a name I adore
to be out and about after billions of years
I was driven to contribute more
now I light the roads at night
image workings of a failing heart
offer strobe lights, propel spaceships, encourage
blood flow — just to do my part

118 known chemical elements arranged
into galaxies, stars and moons
bacteria, every species of life
organizations of different tunes
stars on the table Oxygen and Nitrogen
forget them you wouldn't dare
remember this when you take your next breath
I'm a potent part of your air —

As Is

YES to the snow in May
when the flowers hunger for warmth

YES to the deafening jack hammer
masking a mourning dove's haunting tease

YES to the age spots on my chest
when the body feels ready and strong

YES **[yea-si: so be it]**
a response that fully leans in
no matter what cycles through
for to truly welcome what lands
is to bow to a greater plan

YES to the stench from a garbage truck
when fresh laundry floats on the breeze

YES to unfinished work beckoning
while windows swear outside I belong

YES to chatter about upcoming plans
when this breath is focusing on me

Medicine

We love the movement in a seeming stillness
the breath in the body of the loved one sleeping
the highest leaves in the silent wood
a great migration in the sky above

*– David White, **'A Seeming Stillness'***

FIRE
Spirit who dances without inhibition
celebrating smoking logs that sustain her
still pulsing with energy of originating tree
in the tranquil forest who camouflages
warm bodies occasionally filling
dense air with sweet chirping
a flutter, then motionless again
to bask in the blaze of connected sunrays
we love the movement in a seeming stillness

AIR
Breath so full of emptiness that births
the sigh, the sound, the word, the prayer
an enoughness right here in the silence
that is listening to this life   entering
the space we are made of   to play
with wind moving us when we least expect it
kite tossing up high with its determined tricks
humpback's fountain of joyous rising mist
the breath in the body of a loved one sleeping

WATER
Blood gushing through skin stems with purpose
imitating the rivers after a downpour
when the skies open to teach us
to weep, to flow, to intimately feel
diving into the centre to splash
cupping hands to catch merging drops
till we overflow and must let go
like the veins that carve and glisten on
the *highest leaves in the silent wood*

EARTH
Body holding us together for this lifetime
with *zeal* **[devotion]** she calls out
so I may tune in, let go and drop
into our mother's lap, always here to support
this burn, breath, flow and grounding
even in the quicksand of forgetting
I rescue-write to remembering
constancy within – the One that guides
a great migration in the sky above

Poetry is the verbal artform by which we can actually create silence.

- David Whyte

Acknowledgments

With much gratitude to:

• The Instagram community of poets I have connected with over the past year. This has been a space in which I have shared extracts of my poems, enjoyed prompts/poetry challenges, and developed lovely friendships with other writers in a virtual space filled with positivity! You have warmed my heart and inspired me to keep writing.
IG: @fazila.nurani

• The University of Toronto School of Continuing Studies poetry courses through which I was encouraged and supported in finding my own poetic voice. In particular, I am so thankful for the guidance of instructor Chelene Knight, author of *Dear Current Occupant: A Memoir* who also provided feedback on an early version of this book.

• Members of my monthly poetry workshop group who provided invaluable feedback and suggestions on drafts of some of the poems contained in this book: Bradley Alvarez, Corinna McFarlane, Hayley King, Brenda Gunn and Nancy Daoust.

• The Mythos Poets Society for introducing me to many beautiful poets around the world, and for their continued support of my writing and poetic endeavours.

About the Author

Fazila Nurani was born in Nairobi, Kenya and immigrated to Canada at a very young age. She grew up in Toronto, Canada and now lives north of the city. She has two young adult children and has been practicing law and consulting for over 20 years, specialized in the area of privacy and data protection. Fazila enjoys spending time in the woods behind her home and is a hot yoga lover. She has enjoyed reading, creative writing and painting for as long as she can remember. Fazila derives much satisfaction from balancing an analytical fast-paced career with endeavours that require slowing down. Fazila's poems have appeared in various literary journals, both in print and on-line, and in several poetry anthologies.

photo courtesy of Nicole Quashie

CPSIA information can be obtained
at www.ICGtesting.com
Printed in the USA
LVHW052119210122
708928LV00011B/473